LEA
For being Your Own Best Friend

Edited by
Phil Etienne

Illustrated by
Randy Wollenmann

ONE
CARING
PLACE

Abbey Press
St. Meinrad, IN 47577

MW01596742

Text © 2003 Abbey Press
Illustrations © 2003 St. Meinrad Archabbey
Published by One Caring Place
Abbey Press
St. Meinrad, Indiana 47577

All rights reserved.
No part of this book may be used or reproduced in any
manner without written permission of the publisher,
except in the case of brief quotations embodied in
critical articles and reviews.

Library of Congress Catalog Number
2003101263

ISBN 0-87029-374-5

Printed in the United States of America

Foreword

In a world filled with adversity and strife, we should all have at least one true friend in our corner... ourselves. Whether through a reassuring attitude of self-forgiveness, an internal gauge that alerts us to ease up on a stress-filled lifestyle, or a faith-inspired reminder that "this, too, shall pass"—it's important to take care of that person staring back at us in the mirror each morning. Instead, unfortunately, we are often our own worst critics...the last one to forgive our inequities.

Resist the urge to equate self-esteem and self-care with self-indulgence; and consider, instead, that by loving ourselves, we celebrate the infinite love that the Lord has for us all. From our many publications, we have obtained these morsels of wisdom for caring for oneself, combined them with the greater wisdom of Scripture, and accompanied the brief, thought-provoking insights with adorable illustrations from artist, Randy Wollenmann. May the messages and artwork bring you to a better understanding of what it means to truly care for yourself!

Appreciate the wonders of life. Get in touch with the wide-eyed child within you...be amused at funny things...be awed by the natural splendor that surrounds us...be impressed with the kind acts people perform day in and day out.

"I know that whatever God does endures forever; nothing can be added to it, nor anything taken from it; God has done this, so that all should stand in awe before him."

—Ecclesiastes 3:14

2

Cultivate the habit of happiness. Nurture grateful, happy feelings and let your body speak the language of happiness by putting a spring in your step, a note of pleasure in your voice, and a smile on your face.

"He will yet fill your mouth with laughter, and your lips with shouts of joy."

—Job 8:21

The need for simplicity is a spiritual longing. External things and activities cannot fill internal needs. When you attain simplicity, your sense of trust and control over your life increases.

"Peace I leave with you; my peace I give to you. I do not give to you as the world gives. Do not let your hearts be troubled, and do not let them be afraid."

—John 14:27

Reexamine what you value in life, then begin letting go of unimportant activities.

"It is by your holding fast to the word of life that I can boast on the day of Christ that I did not run in vain or labor in vain."

—Philippians 2:16

Connect with the Source of your being. Each day, take time to pray and meditate. This will help to anchor you in what is real and lasting.

"And why do you worry about clothing? Consider the lilies of the field, how they grow; they neither toil nor spin, yet I tell you, even Solomon in all his glory was not clothed like one of these."

—Matthew 6:28-29

Slow down and focus on one thing at a time. Even a few moments of quiet a day helps put the many elements of your life into perspective.

"I commune with my heart in the night; I meditate and search my spirit..."

—Psalms 77:6

Distinguish the "need" from the "want" in life. Sometimes, deciding to settle for less and feeling good about it can dramatically simplify your life.

"Therefore I tell you, do not worry about your life, what you will eat or what you will drink, or about your body, what you will wear. Is not life more than food, and the body more than clothing?"

—Matthew 6:25

A simple formula for happiness is to <u>want what you have</u>. Feel the richness of what you do have and you'll experience less urgency to keep striving for more.

"Keep your lives free from the love of money, and be content with what you have; for he has said, 'I will never leave you or forsake you.'"

—Hebrews 13:5

Don't let negative emotions destroy you. Making a habit of being preoccupied with dark, gloomy feelings extinguishes the spark of life which allows you to thrive.

"And can any of you by worrying add a single hour to your span of life? If then you are not able to do so small a thing as that, why do you worry about the rest?"

—Luke 12:25-26

Believe that you are good, made in the image of God, and blessed with unique talents. If you believe that you are good, this belief will become the foundation of a relaxed and productive life.

"Then God said, 'Let us make humankind in our image, according to our likeness; and let them have dominion over the fish of the sea, and over the birds of the air, and over the cattle, and over all the wild animals of the earth, and over every creeping thing that creeps upon the earth.'"

—Genesis 1:26

Let love change the course of your world. By graciously giving and receiving love, you will help create a kinder and far more secure world.

"As the Father has loved me, so I have loved you; abide in my love."

—John 15:9

Nurture your emotional and spiritual growth. You will find within yourself the resources necessary to love and grow in the real world.

"What should I do then? I will pray with the spirit, but I will pray with the mind also; I will sing praise with the spirit, but I will sing praise with the mind also."

—1 Corinthians 14:15

Make enthusiasm your daily exercise. Your interactions with others, your work, leisure, prayer, problem-solving time, solitude—each provides you with limitless possibilities for satisfaction in life.

"Render service with enthusiasm, as to the Lord and not to men and women, knowing that whatever good we do, we will receive the same again from the Lord, whether we are slaves or free."

—Ephesians 6:7-8

Give yourself credit for what you have to offer. Instead of getting down on yourself by tallying faults and failings, make a practice of rehearsing your gifts and talents.

"Now we have received not the spirit of the world, but the Spirit that is from God, so that we may understand the gifts bestowed on us by God."

—1 Corinthians 2:12

To fail is human…we do not always do our best. But knowing this truth can help us learn from our failures. They need not overwhelm us or destroy our dreams.

"My flesh and my heart may fail, but God is the strength of my heart and my portion forever."
—Psalms 73:26

click

Failure, in many ways, can be an opportunity. It is an opportunity to congratulate yourself for having tried at all...and opportunity to reevaluate your goals, reassess your direction, and make mid-course corrections.

"In the day of prosperity be joyful, and in the day of adversity consider; God has made the one as well as the other, so that mortals may not find out anything that will come after them."

—Ecclesiastes 7:14

33

Once a day, do something for yourself. Make a list of things that bring you pleasure—for most people, these are surprisingly simple joys.

"Great are the works of the Lord, studied by all who delight in them."

—Psalms 111:2

Take risks! It helps build self-esteem...not because you always get what you go after, but because you grow through facing your fears.

"Prove me, O Lord, and try me; test my heart and mind."

—Psalms 26:2

Believe in your own inner goodness. Look past negative external forces and believe in your own worth...enjoy being who you are.

"...let your adornment be the inner self with the lasting beauty of a gentle and quiet spirit, which is very precious in God's sight."

—1 Peter 3:4

Let go of the desire to be perfect. You might overlook the good within you if you are too preoccupied with wanting everything about yourself and your life to be "a little bit better."

"Better is the sight of the eyes than the wandering of desire; this also is vanity and a chasing after wind."
—Ecclesiastes 6:9

Appreciate all of life's gifts—including your own. The wonders of your body, mind, and spirit can easily be taken for granted. Each day, make an effort to be grateful for one of your easily-taken-for-granted gifts.

"All your works shall give thanks to you, O Lord, and all your faithful shall bless you."

—Psalms 145:10

Discover laughter's healing power. It can be a way to release anxiety and balance distress with healthful, positive feelings.

"Blessed are you who are hungry now, for you will be filled. Blessed are you who weep now, for you will laugh."
—Luke 6:21

Spend time with children. Listen to the peal of a child's laughter and you'll hear sheer joy and love of life. The average four-year-old laughs 500 times a day!

"He called a child, whom he put among them, and said, 'Truly I tell you, unless you change and become like children, you will never enter the kingdom of heaven.'"

—Matthew 18:2-3

Share a funny or embarrassing moment and make a friend. Humor is a universal bond—sharing laughter with friends reminds us that we're not alone and helps overcome awkward moments.

"How very good and pleasant it is when kindred live together in unity!"

—Psalms 133:1

Find out what you're good for. Talent grows out of the unique combination of characteristics that make up who you are. As you cultivate and exercise those special abilities, you'll realize your own potential.

"We have gifts that differ according to the grace given to us: prophecy, in proportion to faith; ministry, in ministering; the teacher, in teaching; the exhorter, in exhortation; the giver, in generosity; the leader, in diligence; the compassionate, in cheerfulness."

—Romans 12:6-8

Go ahead and cry—to relieve stress. Studies have shown that healthy people cry more frequently and feel freer to cry than people who suffer from stress-related illnesses.

"May those who sow in tears reap with shouts of joy."

—Psalms 126:5

Seek balance in your life. The activities of your life are not items to be juggled, but more like elements to be kept in balance, giving each the time it deserves.

"For everything there is a season, and a time for every matter under heaven..."

—Ecclesiastes 3:1

Learn to relax your mind and spirit through prayer and meditation. Any kind of prayer, formal or informal, can bring relaxation—especially if you can give your burdens to God in prayerful offering.

"...strive first for the kingdom of God and his righteousness, and all these things will be given to you as well. So do not worry about tomorrow, for tomorrow will bring worries of its own. Today's trouble is enough for today."

—Matthew 6:33-34

Discover relaxation in the midst of mundane activities by becoming mindful of being totally present to the task at hand. Allow yourself to simply be... relax in God's quiet presence.

"Seek the Lord and his strength; seek his presence continually."

—Psalms 105:4

Seek out hugs daily. The emotional lift you get from hugging and being hugged is a reflection on God's plans for you. You are, after all, a child of a God who loved you into being, a God who took humanity into divine arms.

"I led them with cords of human kindness, with bands of love. I was to them like those who lift infants to their cheeks..."

—Hosea 11:4